DREAM IT.
PIN IT.
LIVE IT.
WORKBOOK

DREAM IT.
PIN IT.
LIVE IT.
WORKBOOK

TERRI SAVELLE FOY

Copyright © 2015 by Terri Savelle Foy
All rights reserved. No part of this publication may be reproduced, distributed, or transmitted in any form or by any means, including photocopying, recording, or other electronic or mechanical methods, without the prior written permission of the publisher, except in the case of brief quotations embodied in critical reviews and certain other noncommercial uses permitted by copyright law. For permission requests, write to the publisher at the address below.

Terri Savelle Foy Ministries
P.O. Box 1959
Rockwall, TX 75087
www.terri.com

Published in association with The Fedd Agency, Inc., a literary agency.

Scripture quotations marked (NIV) are taken from the *Holy Bible, New International Version*®, NIV®. Copyright © 1973, 1978, 1984, 2011 by Biblica, Inc.™ Used by permission of Zondervan. All rights reserved worldwide. www.zondervan.com. The "NIV" and "New International Version" are trademarks registered in the United States Patent and Trademark Office by Biblica, Inc.

Scripture quotations marked NLT are taken from the *Holy Bible*, New Living Translation, copyright ©1996, 2004, 2007, 2013 by Tyndale House Foundation. Used by permission of Tyndale House Publishers, Inc., Carol Stream, Illinois 60188. All rights reserved.

Scripture quotations marked (AMP) are taken from the *Amplified Bible*, Copyright © 1954, 1958, 1962, 1964, 1965, 1987 by The Lockman Foundation. Used by permission.

Scripture quotations marked NASB are taken from the *New American Standard Bible*®, Copyright © 1960, 1962, 1963, 1968, 1971, 1972, 1973, 1975, 1977, 1995 by The Lockman Foundation Used by permission. (www.Lockman.org)

Scripture quotations marked (KJV) are from *The Authorized (King James) Version*. Rights in the Authorized Version in the United Kingdom are vested in the Crown. Reproduced by permission of the Crown's patentee, Cambridge University Press.

Scripture quotations marked (MSG) are from *The Message* copyright © by Eugene H. Peterson 1993, 1994, 1995, 1996, 2000, 2001, 2002. Used by permission of Tyndale House Publishers, Inc.

J. B. Phillips, "The New Testament in Modern English", 1962 edition, published by HarperCollins.

ISBN: 978-1-943217-09-0
Library of Congress Control Number: 2015950123
Cover and Interior Design by Lauren Hall

Printed in the United States of America

First Edition 17 18 19 20 21 / 10 9 8 7 6 5 4 3 2

CONTENTS

Introduction: Using the Workbook..vii

WEEK ONE: Creating the Vision..1
Welcome and discussion of Chapters 1 & 2
Assignment: Start the "101 Dreams" list. Encourage your group to write as many as they can without the pressure of finishing the list.

WEEK TWO: Capturing the Vision..19
Discuss Chapters 3 & 4
Assignment: List your top ten goals for the next 12-18 months. Bring supplies for vision board party at the next gathering.

WEEK THREE: Keeping the Vision..35
Discuss Chapters 5 & 6 at your Vision Board Party
Assignment: Have fun decorating and designing your boards together and share your declarations.

WEEK FOUR: Embracing the Vision..47
Discuss Chapters 7 & 8
Assignment: As a group, share the things you are thanking God for in advance. Establish a network within your group for encouragement and support of those beliefs.

WEEK FIVE: Living the Vision...65
Discuss Chapters 9 & 10
Assignment: Help each other set realistic strategic priorities and share the seed you are sowing. Pray with one another over these goals and be accountable to one another for them, then celebrate together.

WEEK SIX: Expanding the Vision...81
Discuss Chapters 11 & 12
Assignment: Share your inspirational lists and success stories to prepare you for going forward.

APPENDIX: Celebrating the Vision......................................97
Host a Vision Board Party
Vision Board Samples
Gratitude Journal

INTRODUCTION
Using This Workbook

> YOU WILL NEVER LEAVE WHERE YOU ARE
> UNTIL YOU SEE WHERE YOU'D RATHER BE!
> —UNKNOWN

Now that you've read the book, *Dream it. Pin it. Live it.,* you are probably excited and ready to get started. Maybe you are using this workbook on your own; maybe you are using it in a small group gathering. Either way, I am really excited you are taking this big step in reaching for your dreams.

As you know, surrounding yourself with images of your vision causes your dream to become more alive inside you. This vital component of your success will allow you to begin to shift from seeing what is to what can be. That's the power of vision.

The clarity for your dreams and desires you will receive when you create your vision board will help you concentrate and focus on your specific life goals. You will begin to keep your attention on your intentions.

My hope for you as you use this workbook and begin creating your vision board is that you will see yourself the way you want to be. Your vision board will help you on many levels, including:

- prioritizing your goals;
- obtaining clarity in your life purpose;
- building your faith in God's ability to perform the impossible;
- boosting your confidence and self-esteem; and

- reminding you of your mission.

Your vision board will serve as a visual reminder of where you are headed and keep you focused when you are tempted to give up. It keeps you single-minded and full of faith.

Remember: what's in front of you is far more important than what's behind you. Become so focused on where you're going that you won't even consider looking back at where you've been. Paul said in Philippians, "This one thing I do forgetting those things which are behind and reaching for those things which are ahead, I press toward the mark for the prize of the high calling in Christ Jesus." (Philippians 3:13)

In order to reach for what is ahead, you have to be clear on what "those things" are. This workbook and the vision board you create will give you the clarity you need for your dreams and goals. The thoughts raised in the workbook and questions that follow will help you dig in deeper to know what your goals should be and how to work toward them. Each step along the way you will be preparing your heart and mind for creating the vision board that will help you see your future so you can move purposefully toward achieving everything on it. This is an exciting time, and I pray you will have incredible results to share with others for inspiration.

-TERRI

WEEK ONE
CREATING THE VISION

> THERE ARE THREE TYPES OF PEOPLE IN THIS WORLD: THOSE WHO MAKE THINGS HAPPEN, THOSE WHO WATCH THINGS HAPPEN, AND THOSE WHO WONDER WHAT HAPPENED.
>
> —MARY KAY ASH

SECTION ONE

As you begin to dream, you are going to have people tell you you're being foolish or that you're living in a fantasy world. You may even tell yourself that; but, daring to dream—having the audacity to imagine more for yourself—is the only way to move beyond where you are right now.

Destiny Decisions

In Chapter 1 of the book, we talked about destiny decisions as a major factor in getting your life on the right track. Those are choices that have such an impact on your life that they can potentially change the whole direction of your life. So, you definitely don't want to be on the sidelines, allowing those decisions to be made for you!

What do you need to do to make sure you are not just along for the ride in your life? How can you put yourself in the driver's seat to steer your life toward the destination you want and that God wants for you?

_____
_____
_____
_____
_____
_____
_____
_____
_____
_____
_____

One of the greatest realizations you will ever have is knowing there is only one person responsible for the outcome of your life, and it's you. Your decisions affect your destiny!

Are there areas of your life where you have not taken full responsibility for where you are and what is happening? What do you need to change to take ownership of the circumstances in your life and get on the path toward your vision?

_____
_____
_____
_____
_____
_____
_____
_____
_____
_____
_____
_____
_____
_____
_____
_____
_____
_____
_____
_____
_____
_____
_____

Jim Rohn taught that there are certain emotions that can have a huge impact on our drive to change our circumstances. One of the most powerful is disgust. Becoming disgusted with your current circumstances can actually serve as vision and momentum to get you out!

> YOU CANNOT BE WIMPY OUT THERE ON THE DREAM-SEEKING TRAIL. DARE TO BREAK THROUGH BARRIERS TO FIND YOUR OWN PATH.
> —LES BROWN

Have you ever looked around you—at your living conditions, your bank account, your image in the mirror, your influencers—and found yourself feeling disgusted by what you saw? How did you respond to that? Did you turn your eyes away so you didn't have to see it or did it motivate you to do something about what you didn't like?

_____
_____
_____
_____
_____
_____
_____
_____
_____
_____
_____
_____
_____
_____

Don't Settle Where You Are

In Genesis 11:31, we read the story of Abraham's father, Terah, and how he stopped short of where God was leading him. Abraham's father missed out on an unimaginable opportunity God had for him because he settled for much less than God had promised him. Maybe, like the Israelites in Canaan, you thought your dream was taking too long to be realized.

Have you ever stopped dreaming and settled for less? What caused you to quit? What do you think you might have achieved if you hadn't given up?

_____
_____
_____
_____
_____
_____
_____
_____
_____
_____
_____
_____
_____
_____
_____
_____
_____

God is capable of doing impossible things in your life, but you can actually prevent Him from doing them by thinking in terms of "just enough to get by." When you believe the lie that it's better to stay where you are rather than go after what you could be or do, then you will continue to miss out on the abundance God wants to give you.

How often do you settle for less than what you are dreaming of? What would you tell yourself if you were hearing the message that there wasn't a reason to keep going after everything God had in store for you?

_____
_____
_____
_____
_____
_____
_____
_____
_____
_____
_____
_____
_____
_____
_____
_____
_____
_____

You Have the Audacity to Dream That?

Audacity is a powerful word that is often associated with a negative perception of someone, but it can alter the rest of your life if you will be brave enough to embrace it. Audacity is having nerve, courage, daring, boldness, fearlessness, grit, and the willingness to take risks.

Are you ready to be audacious enough to get out of the mundane thinking or the rut you may have found yourself in? What will you have the audacity to dream? What do you have the nerve to believe you can achieve in your life?

You have probably heard the verse in Proverbs 23:7 that says we become what we think about. That is the Law of Attraction summed up in one scripture verse. Whatever gets in your mind and stays there, you will attract in your life.

> A MAN BECOMES WHAT HE THINKS ABOUT MOST OF THE TIME.
> —RALPH WALDO EMERSON

What are you allowing to occupy your mind right now? Are the thoughts you are having regularly something you really want to attract into your life? Where do you want to focus your mind?

_____
_____
_____
_____
_____
_____
_____
_____
_____
_____
_____
_____
_____
_____
_____
_____

Because this principle of attraction is so powerful and where we focus our thoughts has a big impact on our lives, it is important that we get our mind in alignment with God. You will become what you believe.

What do you want to trust God for? Are you believing to live in a particular house, to own your dream business, to weigh an ideal amount, to be healed in your body, or to see the restoration of your family? What are you aligning with God to bring into your life?

_____
_____
_____
_____
_____
_____
_____
_____
_____
_____
_____
_____
_____
_____
_____
_____
_____
_____
_____
_____

Visualizing Success

God said in Isaiah 43:19 (NIV), "See, I am doing a new thing! . . . Do you not perceive it?" He is pouring His favor on you to promote you, increase you, and expand your influence, but He's asking you the question, "Do you see it?"

> I AM ALWAYS DOING THAT WHICH I CANNOT DO, IN ORDER THAT I MAY LEARN HOW TO DO IT.
> —PABLO PICASSO

Do you see where God wants to take you? Are you preparing for more? Do you have a clear vision beyond where you are today?

_____
_____
_____
_____
_____
_____
_____
_____
_____
_____
_____
_____
_____
_____
_____
_____

Your dreams should stretch you, challenge you, and force you to grow in your faith! Hebrews 11:6 says, "It's impossible to please God without faith." That means if your dreams seem impossible, you have no choice but to rely on God to come on the scene and help you. And that's how He wants it. If we leave it up to what we can do on our own, we dream too small.

How can you stretch your dreams further, beyond what you know you can do on your own? What can you reach for that seems ridiculously impossible so you can test your ability to trust God to partner with you on your dream?

_____

_____

_____

_____

_____

_____

_____

_____

_____

_____

_____

_____

_____

_____

WARNING: The number one question that will stop you from dreaming big is asking, "How?" It's not your job to figure out the how. Your job is to dream and dream big.

There's power in just taking time to see beyond where you're at today. Decide where you want to end up in life. Plan your life down to the last detail and then let God go beyond that.

> YOU HAVE TO THINK ANYWAY, SO WHY NOT THINK BIG?
> —DONALD TRUMP

When you think in terms of what would give you the greatest peace in your life, what do you imagine? What does your life look like five years from now?

_____
_____
_____
_____
_____
_____
_____
_____
_____
_____
_____
_____
_____
_____
_____
_____
_____
_____
_____

God has so much more for you than what you presently have. He has given you a unique assignment to complete during your time here on earth, and then it's over. You either turn in the assignment complete or incomplete.

Have you been listening to what God is telling you about His purpose for you? Are you allowing that to become part of your dreams?

_____
_____
_____
_____
_____
_____
_____
_____
_____
_____
_____
_____
_____
_____

> THE TRAGEDY OF LIFE DOES NOT LIE IN NOT REACHING YOUR GOALS. THE TRAGEDY LIES IN NOT HAVING ANY GOALS TO REACH. IT ISN'T A CALAMITY TO DIE WITH DREAMS UNFULFILLED, BUT IT IS A CALAMITY NOT TO DREAM.
> —DR. BENJAMIN MAYS

SECTION TWO

Now that you've begun thinking about what you might dare to dream and opened yourself up to the possibilities, how are you feeling? Are you excited? Scared? Intimidated? Confused? All of those emotions are normal, and if you allow your mind to sit with them too long, you will end up discouraged. That's why it's important to begin creating your vision by writing it down—get it out of your head and in front of you—so you can make it a part of your reality.

> *"And the Lord answered me and said, Write the vision and engrave it so plainly upon tablets that everyone who passes may [be able to] read [it easily and quickly] as he hastens by."*
> —Habakkuk 2:2 (AMP)

Writing Your Dreams & Goals is a Clear Key to Success

Before you design your vision board, you simply need to write. This exercise will force you to clarify what you really want and chart the course for where you want to go. Writing it down enables you to stay focused and more likely to avoid distractions.

What are your heart's desires? What do you really want? When you sit with God and pray for clarity, what is revealed to you?

_____

_____

_____

_____

_____

Without putting your dreams in writing, you will wander year after year, little by little without even realizing it. Similar to what happens when you're at the beach floating in the water and the tide takes you farther and farther away from shore. You suddenly look up and realize how far you've drifted.

> YOU ARE NEVER TOO OLD TO SET ANOTHER GOAL OR TO DREAM A NEW DREAM.
> —C.S. LEWIS

Do you want to wake up one day and wonder, *What have I been doing all these years?* If not, what are you doing to ensure that you don't find yourself off course and miles away from your dreams?

_____
_____
_____
_____
_____
_____
_____
_____
_____
_____
_____
_____
_____
_____

> WHEN YOUR VISION IS CLEAR, THE RESULTS WILL APPEAR!

Start with a few desires of your heart—whatever comes to your mind as you sit still. Open your mind up to the unlimited possibilities that are ahead for you. Using your imagination and without regard for how you can have what you desire, just dream.

Where would you like to travel? What would you like to drive? What would you like to own? How much money would you like to save by December 31st? Where would you like to work? Which university would you like to attend? Who would you like to meet? What does your ideal physical body look like?

_____
_____
_____
_____
_____
_____
_____
_____
_____
_____
_____
_____
_____
_____
_____
_____
_____
_____
_____
_____

Dreams Are Given to You by God

In addition to all the stuff you want, the places you want to see, the adventurous things you want to do, God wants to speak to you about His plan for your life. He cares about all these other things, too. In fact, He is the one who gives us the desires of our hearts. Don't ever think of your dreams and desires as insignificant.

The Bible says that God will give you the desires of your heart. The Latin word for desire means from the father. How do you know when it's a dream from God? When you can't let go of it!

Your vision and your vision board will be unique to you. This is all about your life, your desires and your assignment given by God. Some people get so stuck on deciding what to put on the wall that they don't create a vision board at all. I never start clipping away at photographs in magazines before I first sit quietly with God and dream.

I am giving you a big challenge to write 101 things you want to do with the rest of your life. Don't think about the actual designing of the vision board yet. We will get to that later. First, you need to stretch yourself by thinking.

ACTION STEP
MAKE A LIST OF 101 THINGS YOU WANT TO DO

In creating your vision, you have started by giving yourself permission to dream—to get outside the box and go big. That first step is one of the hardest because it stretches us out of our comfort zones. It means we have to be brave enough to hope for something more and risk disappointment. But, what you will learn through this journey is that there truly is no risk involved because you are believing in your untapped potential and the plans God has for you.

Put a demand on yourself to dream. Let your imagination run wild. They don't all have to be huge, financially expensive or adrenaline-pumping things; just give yourself a reason to get up and do something. You can fill in your list in the space below or create it on a separate piece of paper, but be sure to write it down somewhere.

WEEK TWO
CAPTURING THE VISION

GOALS ARE SIMPLY
DREAMS WITH
DEADLINES

—NAPOLEON HILL

SECTION ONE

In Week 1, we discovered that we have permission to dream and dream big. We also discussed the importance of writing things down to retain them and make them a part of our daily vision. Now that you have a clear idea of what you want to accomplish and where you want to be, it's time to write down your goals. If you've been following along in the book, you may have already written down your goals. If not, take some time to read through the following questions and thoughts before making your list to see if other ideas come up for you or if it affects how you see your goals.

Goals Determine What Drives You!

There probably isn't a person reading this book who hasn't heard the importance of having goals in writing; however, if you walk up to the average person and ask to see their written list of goals, they don't have one! Why do you think people don't follow through on this important step?

> IF YOU'RE BORED WITH LIFE—IF YOU DON'T GET UP EVERY MORNING WITH A BURNING DESIRE TO DO THINGS—YOU DON'T HAVE ENOUGH GOALS.
> —LOU HOLTZ

If you have not written out your goals, think about why not and write down some of the reasons. Once you've done that, write next to them why those excuses should not get in your way and how you can remove them as obstacles from setting your goals.

_____

_____

_____

_____

_____

God wants us to have goals and intermediate objectives that we strive toward each year. We have talked a lot about dreaming big, and that is important; but, it is vital to have smaller dreams (incremental goals) that you can focus on that help move you toward your bigger goals.

> WHERE THERE ARE NO GOALS, NEITHER WILL THERE BE SIGNIFICANT ACCOMPLISHMENTS; THERE WILL ONLY BE EXISTENCE.
> —ANONYMOUS

What are some smaller goals you can add to your list to help you stay on track and focused on the big prize?

_____
_____
_____
_____
_____
_____
_____
_____
_____
_____
_____
_____
_____
_____
_____
_____
_____

Dreams Are Given to You By God

People often get so excited about this process that they tend to set unrealistic goals in the beginning. They might decide they want to become a millionaire in the next year or lose 50 lbs. by swimsuit season when it's already Spring. Setting goals that are too unrealistic, or may take longer than 12-18 months to achieve, sets you up for failure and disappointment.

 I know this may sound contradictory to what I encouraged you to do in dreaming big, but it isn't really. I want you to have high aspirations, but by laying out a roadmap for how to get there that is doable. If you want to lose weight, think about how much is healthy and sustainable to lose in a designated amount of time. If you want to be a millionaire and you are currently in debt and make $30,000 a year, set the target date a little farther out and write out what in your finances and earning potential that you need to change to achieve that goal. Look at your list of goals and consider them from a realistic point of view then revise, if necessary, include achievable steps to keep you moving toward your big goals.

 In the book, we covered the "30-Day Challenge":

1. For the next thirty days, write your ten goals once a day.
2. Write them in the present tense.
3. Write it down each day without looking back to what you wrote yesterday. If you can't remember all ten original goals, that's okay. It just means they weren't all that important to you. Stay focused on the ones that capture your imagination and motivate you to achieve.

Use the space below to write out your Top Ten Goals and use a separate notebook to write them down every day.

1.

2.

3.

4.

5.

6.

7.

8.

9.

10.

Write your Top Ten Goals for this year (or the next 12-18 months).

1.

2.

3.

4.

5.

6.

7.

8.

9.

10.

Goal-Setting S.M.A.R.T. Tips

Let's look more closely at the S.M.A.R.T. goals technique:

Specific: You must bring clarity to what you want to accomplish by being as specific as possible.

Measurable: This is where you can truly measure whether or not you hit a goal.

Action-Oriented: Use action verbs when setting goals, such as: reduce, save, earn, exercise, invest, enroll, run, etc.

Realistic: If your goals are too big, you are setting yourself up to fail. I encourage you to set goals that stretch you and cause you to grow but are also somewhat attainable.

Timeline: Deadlines are motivating. Always establish a "by when" date. It keeps you motivated to achieve it. The most productive day of the year is the day before vacation. Why? There's a deadline. The quickest way to clean your house is to invite company over. Why? There's a deadline.

GOALS ARE NOT ONLY ABSOLUTELY NECESSARY TO MOTIVATE US. THEY ARE ESSENTIAL TO REALLY KEEP US ALIVE.
—ROBERT H. SCHULLER

Use the space below to look at your Top Ten goals and apply the S.M.A.R.T. technique to see if you are on target.

1.

2.

3.

4.

5.

6.

7.

8.

9.

10.

Set a STRETCH Goal

The STRETCH Goal takes you back to the "highest expectation" and "mountain-moving faith" I asked you to tap into to dream big. As you set your smaller goals that you have evaluated under the S.M.A.R.T. technique, look at them again and see if there is anywhere you can stretch yourself. Identify an area you feel is vitally important to you this year and write down a way to reach a little farther than you think you can.

_____
_____
_____
_____
_____
_____
_____
_____
_____
_____
_____
_____
_____
_____
_____
_____

> SETTING GOALS IS THE FIRST STEP IN TURNING THE INVISIBLE INTO THE VISIBLE.
> —TONY ROBBINS

SECTION TWO

Now that you have a clear picture in your head about what you want and realistic goals for how to move you toward those dreams, it's time to start working on putting what is in your mind into pictures on your board that will remind you daily of what you are striving for.

Frame Your Future

When we want to remember the important people in our lives and special times we've spent with them or commemorate things we've previously done and accomplished, we put photographs, certificates, and other mementos in a frame or a scrapbook. A vision board is just the opposite. When you create a vision board, you are literally framing your future before it ever happens!

In the space below write down the reasons you think it is important to "frame your future" in such a way. What benefits do you think you will get from doing this? You might want to think about what picturing your past does for you then compare and contrast those benefits with how it will change your life to frame your future.

_____
_____
_____
_____
_____
_____
_____
_____

The idea is to find images that are a tangible representation of where you want your life to go. Before you go searching, in order to make your time more productive, write down what types of images you want to represent your goals.

_____
_____
_____
_____
_____
_____
_____
_____
_____
_____
_____
_____
_____
_____
_____
_____
_____
_____
_____
_____
_____
_____
_____
_____

Your S.M.A.R.T. Goals in Pictures

Your S.M.A.R.T. goals have an important place on your vision board next to your big dreams because once you start achieving these more attainable goals you will find more motivation to stay focused on the larger dreams for your life.

Referring back to your list of Top Ten Goals for the year find images that illustrate those goals as well. Write your list below again and as you search for images make notes of what makes these goals attainable and how they factor into your bigger dreams.

_____
_____
_____
_____
_____
_____
_____
_____
_____
_____
_____
_____
_____
_____
_____
_____
_____
_____

When we get too many items on the board, it can create a snapshot of confusion, so being selective is essential. Arrange your photos and your goals in an order that appeals to you. I prefer to have giant numbers next to each of my ten goals for the year.

Use the space below to experiment with different designs and sketch the layout of your vision board so you have an organized approach to it before you start gluing or pinning things to your board.

Special Occation and Theme Boards

Some people have several vision boards that represent specific themes or special occasions. Your board doesn't just have to be for the great aspirations of your life's purpose. What other goals or ambitions do you have? Are you planning for a big wedding? A special family vacation? A new home? Write in the space below some themes or special occasions that might need a vision board for you to more effectively work toward them.

_____
_____
_____
_____
_____
_____
_____
_____
_____
_____
_____
_____
_____
_____
_____
_____
_____
_____

No matter your dream, it is important to have a clear vision of what it will take to achieve it. Think about what it will take—budget, resources, time, etc.—to make these goals happen and write those items down as well.

_____
_____
_____
_____
_____
_____
_____
_____
_____
_____
_____
_____
_____
_____
_____
_____
_____
_____
_____
_____
_____
_____
_____

ACTION STEP
TAKE THE "10/30 GOALS CHALLENGE"

You may (or may not) want to look over your extensive list created in Chapter 2 to pull ideas from. If you choose to sift through this list, narrow it down to what you feel is most important at this time in your life. It can include financial goals, family goals, physical goals, career goals. They can be as big or as small as you want as long as you feel that is has a 50% chance of happening.

- Use a notebook.
- Write your Top Ten Goals for this year (or the next 12-18 months).
- For the next thirty days, write your ten goals once a day.
- Write them in the present tense.
- Write it down each day without looking back to what you wrote yesterday.

Review the S.M.A.R.T. goals technique as you're listing them.

Imagine it is December 31st, and you joyfully exclaim, "This has been the most amazing year of my life!" What needs to happen in order for you to say that? Write those goals down.

WEEK THREE
KEEPING THE VISION

> THE MIND HAS A MIRACULOUS ABILITY TO FIGURE OUT WAYS OF ACHIEVING WHAT IT THINKS ABOUT MOST.
>
> —BILL CHANDLER

SECTION ONE

Remember, we discussed the importance of keeping your vision in front of you constantly. It won't happen if you put it in a drawer and forget about it until the next time someone mentions a vision board to you. Not only is it important to remind yourself daily of what you are working toward, you should be proud of what you are setting out to accomplish. Keep yourself motivated and accountable.

You Are Transformed into the Image Before Your Eyes

The more you look at the images of your ideal future, the more you desire them. The more you desire them, the more persistent you become in fulfilling them. Keep your visual reminder of what you are expecting to accomplish before you where it is easily accessible to you and ever-present before your eyes.

Where will you place your board? What tools can you use to remind yourself daily of your goals? Will a calendar alert help? What about an app like the one we offer at www.terri.com? Use the space below to write down ideas of how to keep your vision board in front of you in a practical way.

_____
_____
_____
_____
_____
_____
_____

You Become What You Behold

Joshua 1:8 tells us to behold the Word of God (do not let the Word depart from your eyes; keep them in the midst of your heart). Just as with God's Word, your vision for your future needs to be meditated on—think deeply or focus your mind for a period, to engage in reflection—day and night. As you meditate on your vision, it might be helpful to keep a journal close by to record any revelations or ideas that come during your time of reflection.

If you don't want to keep a journal, you can use the space below to write down some of the thoughts that come up in your meditation or prayer time.

This Was God's Idea

The concept of visualization and meditation is not just for new age spiritualism. In fact, God came up with it first! He wants us to spend time contemplating what we want from life and where we focus our energy and attention. He told us in the Bible that "as a man thinks, so is he." From that message, do you believe there is any doubt that He wants us to keep our minds focused on things that are useful and productive? Your vision board will help you do this.

What thoughts have you been having that are distracting you from accomplishing your goals or fulfilling God's purpose for your life? How will getting a clear picture of what you want to achieve help you redirect those thoughts?

_____
_____
_____
_____
_____
_____
_____
_____
_____
_____
_____
_____
_____
_____

Look Beyond Current Circumstances

It is not unusual to feel overwhelmed and bogged down in your life. To move past this place, you need to stop looking at what is around and thinking this is as good as it gets. Surrounding yourself with what *can be* in your life will help you see beyond your present circumstances.

You've begun designing your dream board, so you have in mind what you want for your future. What things do you need to change about the way you are seeing your life right now in order to start achieving your dreams? What are you telling yourself about what is that might be distracting or discouraging you about what can be?

_____
_____
_____
_____
_____
_____
_____
_____
_____
_____
_____
_____
_____
_____
_____
_____

The Importance of Visualizing

Visualization is the use of the imagination through pictures or mental imagery to create a vision of what we want in our lives. You actually visualize quite often but probably aren't aware that's what you are doing. When you're hungry, you visualize what you want to eat. When you plan a vacation, you visualize where you want to go. God even said, in reference to the men building the tower of Babel, "This is only the beginning of what they will do. Now, nothing they have imagined they can do will be impossible for them." If you can visualize it, that's the first step in doing it.

Take some time to sit quietly, alone with God. Close your eyes and see yourself attaining every dream God has put in your heart. Clearly see the outcome you desire. Use the space below to write down the emotions you are feeling as you experience this dream. Describe who is with you, what you are wearing, what your environment is like.

_____
_____
_____
_____
_____
_____
_____
_____
_____
_____
_____
_____

SECTION TWO

Now that you understand the importance of visualizing your dreams and, even more important, visualizing yourself achieving your dreams, it is vital to put that into motion in a meaningful way. As you prepare to move forward, you may run into mental roadblocks that threaten to derail your progress. The messages we tell ourselves can have an enormous impact on our ability to take the necessary steps to reach our goals.

What's Coming Out of Your Mouth Has Everything To Do With What You Are Experiencing

Your vision board is now designed, your goals are clear, and your dreams are imagined. And you are probably wondering, *Now what?* You need to focus on the words you use in connection with your dreams. If you are allowing negative self-talk about your life, you must replace it with positive declarations affirming your future. Your words are a tool to be used to help you reach your goals.

Take some time to think about any negative thoughts that may have come up when you were making your list of goals. Did you allow any of these to limit yourself in what you believed God was impressing on your heart? Did you say, "this is impossible" or "I'm not good enough for that?" Use the space below to write down the negative things that came up for you.

_____

_____

_____

_____

_____

_____

One of the greatest things you can do to see the images on your vision board come to life is speak them out of your mouth. It is vitally important that you silence the negative "mind chatter" taking place from the moment you wake up until you go to bed. When your negative thoughts are entertained in your mind long enough, they will eventually start coming out of your mouth. Matthew 12:34 says,". . . for out of the overflow of the heart the mouth speaks."

Now take that list of negative thoughts you just wrote down and turn them into an affirmation of your dreams. Either change the wording so they are positive or write a response that rejects that negative message.

_____
_____
_____
_____
_____
_____
_____
_____
_____
_____
_____
_____
_____
_____
_____
_____

Your words have the ability to destroy and the power to build up. Your words have power. It's not okay to be critical of yourself. Start asking yourself, "Is what I'm about to say what I want to come about in my life?" If it does not line up with your dreams on that board, then don't voice it.

> IF YOU'LL CHANGE WHAT YOU'RE SAYING, YOU'LL CHANGE WHAT YOU'RE SEEING.
> —JOEL OSTEEN

Below, write a list of positive things you want to say to yourself every day. You can use the list of positive responses to your negative thoughts or you can create a whole new list of positive and encouraging messages to yourself. Keep the list available so you can incorporate it into your daily routine.

_____
_____
_____
_____
_____
_____
_____
_____
_____
_____
_____
_____
_____
_____
_____

> IT'S ONE THING TO STOP SAYING THE WRONG THINGS, BUT YOU'VE GOT TO START SAYING THE RIGHT THINGS.
> —JOYCE MEYER

Here are three powerful keys to position you to live the very dreams on your vision board:

#1. Declare God's promises over your life.
Declaring God's promises over your life is one of the most powerful things you can ever do. What you repeatedly hear, you will eventually believe. When you consistently hear uplifting, positive declarations spoken from your own mouth about your future, you will get in agreement with it, and eventually experience it!

#2. Declare your unique, individual desire.
Eliminate all the negative words that are trapping you into the very things you don't want, and replace those words with positive declarations of where you want to be. Changing the way you speak, you will improve your level of confidence, boost your self-esteem, increase your courage, and see positive results unfold.

#3. Declare your dreams.
Some dreams will never manifest in your life until you begin speaking them out loud. Remember, take a proactive approach to your dreams! Speak them out BEFORE they happen!

In the space below, write out ways you can begin using these keys in your own life.

_____
_____
_____
_____
_____

Use this list of Bible verses for inspiration and reflection to help you begin speaking God's promises over your dreams:

"I will be strong and not give up, for my work will be rewarded." (2 Chronicles 15:7)

"God is giving me the desires of my heart and making all my plans succeed." (Psalm 20:4)

"I delight myself in the Lord, and he will give me the desires of my heart." (Psalm 37:4-5)

"I trust in the Lord with all my heart and lean not on my own understanding; in all my ways, I acknowledge Him and He shall direct my path." (Proverbs 3:6)

"I commit to the Lord whatever I do, and he will establish my plans." (Proverbs 16:3)

"I do not remember the former things nor consider the things of old, behold, God is doing a new thing in my life and now it shall spring forth." (Isaiah 43:18-19)

"I can do all this through him who gives me strength." (Philippians 4:13)

"I will not throw away my confidence; it will be richly rewarded." (Hebrews 10:35)

"I throw off everything that hinders and the sin that so easily entangles me. I run with perseverance the race marked out for me, fixing my eyes on Jesus." (Hebrews 12:1)

"God gives strength to the weary and increases power to the weak." (Isaiah 40:29)

"I am strong in the Lord and in his mighty power." (Ephesians 6:10)

"His grace is sufficient for me and strength is made perfect in weakness." (2 Corinthians 12:9)

"God knows the plans He has for me, plans for welfare and not evil, to give me a future and a hope." (Jeremiah 29:11)

ACTION STEP

#1. Make a list of positive declarations to speak over yourself. Start with the words I AM. These are power words. Your spirit takes any sentence that begins with "I am" as a command. It is a directive to make happen.

#2. Structure your declaration in the present tense. State what you are expecting in the present tense as if it is already yours.

#3. State your dream in the positive. Always state your declarations in the positive form. Avoid the negative focus such as: "I'm losing weight." "I'm not in debt." Instead say things such as: "I am debt-free." "I am at my perfect weight of 125 pounds."

#4. Speak them out consistently. Set an alarm on your phone (if needed) in order to develop this habit in your life. You will get to a place in your daily routine where you no longer need to be reminded, you just do it. The more you do it, the more you begin to memorize your declarations and they just start pouring out of your mouth.

The best way to start a habit is to do it at the same time each day. I recommend starting and ending your day speaking to your future. It doesn't take long, it just takes consistency.

Warning: Simply reading words on a piece of paper or staring at a vision board and reading your dreams in a robotic tone is not going to change your circumstances. You must believe it. There is power in your mouth. Make a list of the positive changes you want to see in your life, and start speaking them out consistently.

WEEK FOUR
KEEPING THE VISION

> GRATITUDE IS A POWERFUL PROCESS. THE ONLY WAY TO MOVE TO THE NEXT LEVEL IS YOU MUST SHOW GRATITUDE FOR WHERE YOU ARE. IF YOU SHOW GRATITUDE, IT GETS YOU TO WHERE YOU WANT TO BE QUICKER.
>
> —STEVE HARVEY

SECTION ONE

When you change the way you look at things, the things you look at will change! Gratitude produces the Law of Attraction in action. Gratitude can instantly transform your life. No matter where you are in life, you have something to be grateful for. As soon as you recognize it and express it, your life will start to improve.

Barriers to Attracting What You Need

Most people do not realize that focusing on what they do not have only causes them to attract never having it. When we find fault with and voice our complaints about our lives, we are actually creating an environment to receive more of what we are complaining about. What you think about, you continue to bring about.

What conditions are you experiencing year after year with no progress? Are you complaining about your metabolism, your lazy spouse, your rebellious children, your lousy job, your inability to lose weight, your lingering debts, your low-paying job, etc.? In the space below, write down some ways you can start thinking differently about these situations.

_____

_____

_____

_____

_____

_____

_____

_____

The Bible does not say, "Be thankful and think so." It says, "Be thankful and *say* so." We are clearly instructed to voice our gratitude and appreciation. You've probably been told most of your life to "count your blessings." Truly, when you express appreciation for what you already have, it multiplies.

Start now by writing down a list of the things you are grateful for in your life today. This is a practice you will want to have for every day, but start right now, no matter how hectic your day was or what went wrong. Write down what was good and what went right today.

Whatever You Focus on Expands

The more you voice your dissatisfaction or discontent with your situation, the more you attract those things into your life. But, if you exchange your complaints for positive declarations and expressions of gratitude, thanking the Lord for His promises, the more you will reverse your situation.

If your concern is weight loss, what can you do to change your physical appearance? If your concern is for your finances, what can you do to change how you handle money? What will expressing gratitude change about the way you see and approach these things?

_____
_____
_____
_____
_____
_____
_____
_____
_____
_____
_____
_____
_____
_____
_____
_____
_____

Vital Key - You Must Feel It!

The idea behind the gratitude principle is that by expressing feelings of gratitude, you'll literally feel more blessed and thereby attract more abundance into your life. As you begin to practice gratitude, look at how areas in your life change as a result. This will be an ongoing process, but a shift in attitude usually provides some immediate results.

Write down how you feel about the possibilities for improving your situation just by writing down your gratitude list.

When you begin expressing gratitude, especially when your circumstances are less than pleasant, you're likely to begin trying your best to look on the "bright side," using "at least" expressions in an attempt to build some sort of positive momentum. But, these statements reflect that, deep down, you're not that thrilled about seeing things positively. Gratitude means you stop focusing on what you don't have and start focusing on what you do have. It is one of the most positive emotions we have.

What in your life can you identify that isn't just an "at least" scenario, but is truly a blessing you need to acknowledge? What little things in your life can you recognize so they begin adding up to big gratitude?

_____
_____
_____
_____
_____
_____
_____
_____
_____
_____
_____
_____
_____
_____
_____
_____

Gratitude Gives God an Opportunity to Show Off!

In order to get past the "at least" perspective and shift into real gratitude, you absolutely must feel as if you already have what you pinned on that vision board! That means fists clinched, wide smiled, squealing with exhilaration because you know it's done! When you praise God with that much enthusiasm, it gets His attention.

Pick one of your goals/dreams and identify how you would feel if your dream manifested today. Write your expression of joy and gratitude below.

The 24-Hour Test

In order to launch this attitude of gratitude, let's do a test. Start with one day—one full day of expressing your heartfelt gratitude for everything. This means no complaining whatsoever. For an entire day, start saying, "Thank You, Lord" for anything and everything. You will be utterly amazed at how a simple shift in your attitude from complaining to expressing gratitude can bring such fulfillment, absolute relief from stress and anxiety, appearance of blessings, an atmosphere of peace, the presence of God, strength in your body and the realization of your dreams.

After completing your 24-Hour Test, come back to this space and record what you experienced. What changes did you see in your attitude and the way you dealt with others, how you handled stress or unexpected demands? How did it impact how your day went?

_____
_____
_____
_____
_____
_____
_____
_____
_____
_____
_____
_____

The Highest Expression of Your Faith

Now, take it a step further and start thanking God in advance for what He is about to do in your life. This is the highest expression of your faith. This offering of praise and thanksgiving for what you are desiring touches the heart of God. Your life will never change until you begin vocalizing what you believe God intends to do for you and through you. When you praise and thank God, you are activating your faith and doing exactly what God's Word tells you to do.

What things can you thank God for in advance? What are the desires of your heart that you can believe God is working to bring about in your life?

_____
_____
_____
_____
_____
_____
_____
_____
_____
_____
_____
_____
_____
_____
_____
_____
_____

If you really believe you receive when you pray, then go ahead and take it a step further, and act the part! Talk like a person who has already achieved their dream. Walk confidently like a person who has attained success. Dress like a person who lives the life you desire to live. This demonstration of faith will create positive expectancy at a whole new level.

What can you do to change the way you act and function in your daily life so it reflects what you believe God is doing in your life?

_____
_____
_____
_____
_____
_____
_____
_____
_____
_____
_____
_____
_____
_____
_____
_____
_____

SECTION TWO

One of the most important decisions we make in life is choosing our friendships. Your success can be determined in part by those you surround yourself with, but it can also be determined by who you do not allow in your space. Small-minded people have a way of sucking ambition right out of you. Big minds have a way of elevating you to reach your highest potential. Who you share your dreams with makes a difference in your ability to achieve those dreams. Who you spend your time with has a huge impact on the dreams you achieve.

Who is in Your Sphere of Influence?

God will strategically place people in your life to inspire you to come up higher. Your enemy, Satan, will also strategically place people in your life to pull you down. We all need to make assessments of the people we are spending most of our time with and how they may be affecting our lives. Consider what type of impact your various relationships have on your pursuit of what God has put in your heart.

Who in your life is inspiring you to come up higher? Who in your life is pulling you down?

_____

_____

_____

_____

_____

_____

_____

You can take control over the influences in your life. You can choose your connections based on people you admire, respect and want to be more like. If you're ready to go after the big dreams and goals God has put in your heart, then it's also time to take a close look at the people you're surrounded by.

Ask yourself, who should I share my dreams with? Will they laugh at my vision board? Will they snicker and sarcastically reply, "In your dreams!"? Will they show disinterest in my ambitions because they think it's a waste of time or out of reach for "people like us"?

> THERE JUST AREN'T ENOUGH HOURS IN THE DAY TO WASTE TIME INTERACTING WITH PEOPLE WHO ARE NOT FOCUSED, DRIVEN AND IN SOME WAY HELPING YOU ACHIEVE YOUR GOALS.
> —NIGEL BOTTERILL

Just as you have to choose who you will share your dreams with, it is equally important to determine who doesn't get access to that important part of your life. Below is a list of people who do not need to see your vision board or share in your dreams:

#1. Negative Thinkers—pessimistic in their outlook, find only problems and no solutions, unable to get past what looks difficult to see what can be. Do you know any negative thinkers? How can you minimize their influence?

_____
_____
_____
_____
_____
_____
_____

#2. Sleepwalkers—settled for mediocrity, lacking focus, and content to work, eat, sleep, repeat, on autopilot and do not see beyond today—sleepwalking through life. Do you know any sleepwalkers? How can you minimize their influence?

_____
_____
_____
_____
_____
_____
_____

#3. Negative Talkers—always expressing negative thoughts such as doubts, frustrations, complaints, don't have kind words to say, are toxic in their attitude. Do you know any negative talkers? How can you minimize their influence?

_____
_____
_____
_____

#4. Gossipers—more concerned about what others are doing than what they are doing themselves, like to talk about other people's troubles or failures. Do you know any gossipers? How can you minimize their influence?

_____
_____
_____
_____

#5. Dream Thieves—don't contribute to or support your dreams, may put you and your dreams down or tell you you'll never achieve them, steal encouragement and excitement. Do you know any dream thieves? How can you minimize their influence?

_____
_____
_____
_____

Intentional Friendships

Since who you spend time with influences who you become, you may need some new relationships in your life. If you invest your time with successful, positive-minded friends, you will become a more proactive goal-achiever.

> *"If you walk with wise men, you'll become wise. But the companion of fools will be destroyed."*
> *—(Proverbs 13:20 paraphrased)*

Consider the people in your life who are positive and uplifting. How can you spend more time with them and have more of their influence in your life?

_____
_____
_____
_____
_____
_____
_____
_____
_____
_____
_____
_____
_____
_____
_____

Connect with people who have skills and qualities that you admire and want to emulate in your life. Yes, it requires more confidence and may be a bit uncomfortable to surround yourself with quality people, but that means you're growing. As long as you're comfortable, you're not growing.

> IF YOU'RE AT THE HEAD OF THE CLASS, YOU'RE IN THE WRONG CLASS.
> —JOHN MAXWELL

Success Is Contagious

The company you keep reflects your personality. Who you choose to surround yourself with speaks of your values. You are the mirror reflection of your influencers. Want to be successful? Surround yourself with successful people.

SO, WHO ARE YOUR "FIVE"? Make a list of the five people (closest friends) you are surrounded by.

1.
2.
3.
4.
5.

Identify at least one quality you admire most about each one.

1.
2.
3.
4.
5.

On a scale of 1-10, how ambitious would you rate them?

1.
2.
3.
4.
5.

Just as you become like the people you spend the most time with, you also transform into the persons you spend the most time listening to and learning from. Being exposed to their teaching is similar to interacting with them. Find people who inspire you, encourage you, build your faith and challenge you to grow. In summary, be selective about your closest associations. Choose, on purpose, to surround yourself with greatness and you, too, will become great.

ACTION STEP
CREATE A GRATITUDE JOURNAL

Share things you are thanking God for in advance. Seek out relationships with people who have qualities you desire. Establish a strong network of like-minded dreamers for encouragement and support of those beliefs. In the back of the book, you will find a journaling section. Use that to write about all the things you are grateful for.

WEEK FIVE
LIVING THE VISION

> IF YOU WANT TO BE SUCCESSFUL, STUDY SUCCESSFUL PEOPLE. IF YOU WANT TO BE RICH, STUDY RICH PEOPLE. IF YOU WANT TO BE SKINNY, STUDY SKINNY PEOPLE.
>
> —DAVE RAMSEY

SECTION ONE

While you are waiting patiently for these dreams and goals to manifest in your life, you may feel time is ticking away and nothing is changing. It can be difficult to stay optimistic when it seems you are treading water and not progressing. Focus is essential while you are waiting for your dreams to take shape.

The Secret of Your Future Is in Your Daily Routine

Let's look at that again: The secret of your future is in your daily routine. In other words, you can find clues to why you are or are not successful in how you use the time available in your day. The bottom line is this, if you want more, you must become more. If you are allowing too many distractions in your day to keep you from your maximum productivity, you are responsible for the state of your life. If you have laser focus on a few things that matter, you will accomplish more.

Consider your schedule, look at your calendar if you need to, and be honest about how much time you wasted on things that didn't matter. What activities consume your time without contributing to your goals? What do you need to add to your daily routine to help you progress?

_____
_____
_____
_____
_____
_____
_____

Who Do You Need to Become to Achieve Your Goal?

What you achieve isn't nearly as important as who you become as you're working on a worthy goal. As you're working on a goal, the goal is working on you. Successful people never stop growing.

In what areas of your life do you need to spend time growing and developing yourself further?

HABIT #1: FOCUS ON LISTENING — The first habit to adapt into your new routine is the habit of listening to faith-building, motivational teaching. This very well could be the missing ingredient you need to see your dreams come to pass. You need faith to achieve your dreams. This practice of building your faith needs to be incorporated into your daily routine. Your faith level has to rise to meet your dream level.

How can you increase your faith? What habits can you incorporate to test your faith muscles?

_____
_____
_____
_____
_____
_____
_____
_____
_____
_____
_____
_____
_____
_____
_____
_____
_____
_____
_____

HABIT #2: FOCUS ON READING — The next habit that will make a difference is committing to a quest for continual growth. Do something to continually educate yourself such as reading for twenty minutes each day. In the beginning, it may feel like this does not help you make progress, but keep at it. Every day matters. Every inch of progress is still progress.

Make a list of books, articles, or blogs that relate to your goals or at least are of interest to you. Start by giving yourself twenty minutes each day for reading and stick with it. Even if you only get through a chapter a day, eventually you will finish the book! So what if it takes two weeks, a month, or longer to finish a book? At least you read it!

> YOU CAN'T HIRE SOMEBODY ELSE TO DO YOUR PUSH-UPS!
> —JIM ROHN

_____
_____
_____
_____
_____
_____
_____
_____
_____
_____
_____
_____
_____
_____
_____

HABIT #3: FOCUS ON THREE PRIORITIES — Achieving success requires narrowing our focus by recognizing the distractions that are pulling on us. You may have heard the phrase that it's better to be world class at a few things than mediocre at most things. Identifying three strategic priorities will help you target the best places to focus your time and energy.

What can you focus on that will help you become world class at the dream you're most passionate about? What are your three strategic priorities?

> IF YOU HAVE MORE THAN THREE PRIORITIES, YOU DON'T HAVE ANY.
> —JIM COLLINS

_____
_____
_____
_____
_____
_____
_____
_____
_____
_____
_____
_____
_____
_____
_____
_____
_____

HABIT #4: FOCUS ON ONE AT A TIME — Focus on one priority at a time. If you are trying to do more than one thing at a time, it isn't likely that you will do any of them as well as you could. Don't allow lack of focus to paralyze you in inefficiency. There will always be an unlimited list of goals we need to accomplish, and priorities are always fighting for our attention; but, if we want to reach our goals, we must learn how to strategically say no.

> THE ONLY WAY TO GET AHEAD IS TO GET BETTER. IF YOU'RE NOT CONTINUALLY IMPROVING IN THE MOST IMPORTANT AREAS, THEN YOU'RE NOT MOVING AHEAD.
> —DARREN HARDY

In which area do you need to get laser-focused? What can you say no to, even if it's just temporarily?

_____
_____
_____
_____
_____
_____
_____
_____
_____
_____
_____
_____
_____
_____
_____
_____

God Can't Use You Publicly Until... You've Gotten Victory Privately!

God sees everything. He sees the sacrifices you make, the work you are doing to grow, all the effort you are putting forth to become more. Preparation time is never wasted time.

> SUCCESS IS THE SUM OF SMALL EFFORTS REPEATED DAY IN AND DAY OUT.
> —ROBERT COLLIER

Determine today that you will gain and maintain good habits that others will admire, that God will promote and that will lead you to prosperity and success.

What areas can you identify where you need to develop and grow more? What can you do to help you prepare for receiving the blessings that come with achieving your goals?

SECTION TWO

You may be wondering how you will you ever attain what you need to accomplish your big dreams. You may be wondering how others get where they are when they started with so little. The people who succeed at reaching their highest dreams are those who have tapped into the hidden key known as the power of giving. Many people who have a dream, especially a financial dream, think it's best to hold tight to what they have; but, in reality, it is wise to release it. When you give to the Kingdom of God, you are opening the door for God to give you back more.

God's System of Finance Never Fails

When you give, it positions you to receive more in your life. Your giving represents your faith in your future. It creates opportunities for God to bless you and multiply what you have to work with. When you get involved in building God's dream, He will get involved in building yours.

Are you giving all you could or are you holding back? How can you make room to give more?

_____
_____
_____
_____
_____
_____
_____
_____
_____

There are natural consequences to our acts of giving. It sows a seed for a future harvest. If you know exactly what you're giving for, you'll recognize the harvest when it comes.

We reap in kind to what we sow. However, just expressing gratitude for the seeds will not produce results. You must sow for each of your dreams if you want a harvest in your life.

What are you sowing for? What harvest are you hoping to yield?

_____
_____
_____
_____
_____
_____
_____
_____
_____
_____
_____
_____
_____
_____
_____
_____
_____
_____
_____

Give to Someone Else's Dream

When you invest in someone else's dream, you actually help yourself more than you help them. You strategically put yourself in a position to receive from God! It's not about giving just so you can get. God wants to see that we are honoring Him by helping others and that we are trusting Him to take care of our needs by not holding back when we help others.

> IT IS ONE OF THE BEAUTIFUL COMPENSATIONS OF THIS LIFE THAT NO MAN CAN SINCERELY TRY TO HELP ANOTHER WITHOUT HELPING HIMSELF.
> —RALPH WALDO EMERSON

Where do you see God urging you to sow seeds in someone else's dream? What can you do to encourage another person to strive for more and realize their purpose?

You Can't Out Give God

We are the most like God when we give! The desire you have to help others is something God put in you, and when you obey that prompting, you actually help yourself. God never forgets a seed sown. When you give tithes and offerings to God, it is one of the best guarantees of prosperity ever known!

How many times have you given an offering or made a charitable donation without thinking about what you're "sowing that seed" for? Decide exactly what you need, and then turn it into a seed.

Give More to Receive More

We receive, in life, proportionately to what we give. It really is a simple principle: the more you give, the more you receive. But, never give under pressure. God is more interested in your heart than the amount of money you're giving.

Have you ever given begrudgingly or out of obligation? If you find yourself with that attitude, what can you do to adjust your heart so the seed you sow is given with the right intention?

We all want that harvest in our lives, but often we want it ahead of God's timing. We want instant results or else we declare that it isn't working. Never allow yourself to get jealous over someone else who could be in the "harvest season" while you are still in the "planting season". Just remember that they also had to plant and wait. Let their results encourage you with confidence that you are next in line.

How can you encourage yourself to stay the course and be patient for God's timing? What tools or habits will help you stay focused on the work you are doing so you can trust the work God is also doing to bring about your harvest?

_____
_____
_____
_____
_____
_____
_____
_____
_____
_____
_____
_____
_____
_____
_____
_____

ACTION STEP

CREATE A DONATION LIST AND NAME YOUR SEEDS SOWN

I want to challenge you to put a demand on your faith in God by giving a financial gift or sowing a seed of some kind for each and every one or your dreams. It could be one large donation for all of your dreams, or individual gifts for each dream. There is no right or wrong way to invest in your dreams.

Let God speak to you about what to give and where to give it. Listen to His instruction for your finances. Hearing His voice is the best assurance of receiving the harvest He desires for you to have. The point is, if you're down to your last dollar, don't hold on to it, sow it. Plant that financial seed in the ground and watch God multiply it.

WEEK SIX
EXPANDING THE VISION

> INSPIRATION EXISTS,
> BUT IT HAS
> TO FIND US WORKING.
>
> —PABLO PICASSO

SECTION ONE

It doesn't matter how big or small your list of goals, plans, and activities are. The focus should be on your zest for living life to the fullest and fulfilling every dream God has put in your heart to do. Planning the highlights of your life, living on purpose, removing limitations, and maximizing your moments will enable you to create a vision board and a vision that takes you beyond anything you could imagine.

Below you will find some ideas for lists you can create to help you continue to develop your vision. Pick five of them to start and fill in responses. Once you have your lists, look over them and use them to add to your vision board or create theme-related boards for your dreams. Try to keep your responses to no more than ten. Listing too many things will keep you from being focused.

#1. Countries you would like to visit.
#2. Things you would like to collect.
#3. Activities you would like to try.
#4. Beaches you would like to visit (and collect sand).
#5. Monuments you would like to see.
#6. Books you would like to read.
#7. Plays you would like to see.
#8. Classes you would like to take.
#9. Museums you would like to visit.
#10. Parades you would like to view.
#11. A language(s) you would like to learn.
#12. States you would like to visit.
#13. Special events you would like to witness.
#14. Celebrities you would like to meet.
#15. Organizations you would like to support.
#16. Creative dates you would like to have.
#17. Adventures you'd like to experience.
#18. Creative projects you'd like to try.
#19. Personal or family growth opportunities you'd like to explore.
#20. Charitable and volunteer activities you'd to participate in.

List #1

1.
2.
3.
4.
5.
6.
7.
8.
9.
10.

List #2

1.
2.
3.
4.
5.
6.
7.
8.
9.
10.

List #3

1.
2.
3.
4.
5.
6.
7.
8.
9.
10.

List #4

1.
2.
3.
4.
5.
6.
7.
8.
9.
10.

List #5

1.
2.
3.
4.
5.
6.
7.
8.
9.
10.

SECTION TWO

In the book, I shared stories from people who have written to me about their dreams and goals, what they did to work toward them, and how they were realized. Each one was inspiring in its own way.

Permission to Dream – A Vision for a Horse Farm

Pam from North Carolina shared that her dream began when she was just trying to survive and thought just having a house was a pretty big dream, but was encouraged to go bigger. Without actually thinking it would work, she added a horse farm to her vision board. The dream went with her to other homes as she moved around, but eventually one of the places she moved was to that horse farm that was her wildest dream. Pam is a great example of how we shouldn't limit ourselves or God when we start creating our vision boards.

Have you been limiting yourself by saying, "That's not realistic," or "I can't imagine how that could ever happen"? What can you tell yourself instead to give yourself permission to dream bigger?

_____
_____
_____
_____
_____
_____
_____
_____
_____

Clarity Is Key – A Vision for TV Equipment

The church in Bristol, UK shared their story of being really specific with their list of dreams, itemizing what they needed to accomplish their goal for a TV studio. The clarity that came from seeing exactly what they needed on their board allowed them to be attuned to what was being provided for them and to keep moving toward their goal.

Have you been specific and clear about your goals? What more can you do to bring more clarity to your goals?

The "30-Day Challenge" – A Vision for a Mission Trip and New Job

Mary from North Carolina had a vision for a mission trip and a new job. She told us how she kept her dreams and goals in front of her, going over them and praying about them daily. She stuck with the principle of the "30-Day Challenge" and was amazed by what came to pass in that time.

Do you see the benefits of the "30-Day Challenge" and how it can help you in visualizing your dreams? How will you put this principle into action in your own life?

_____
_____
_____
_____
_____
_____
_____
_____
_____
_____
_____
_____
_____
_____
_____
_____
_____

What Goes on Your Board – A Vision for a Kidney

Celia from Florida tells us about the experience a friend had in believing for a new kidney. Andre's mom created a dream journal and a vision board where she put a picture of a kidney for her son. That might seem like an unusual thing to go on a vision board, but it was the dream they had after waiting for so long. Remember: your dreams can be anything you think will create greater opportunities for you and that you think God wants for your life. Don't restrict yourself and don't limit God. Put those images everywhere they need to be to keep you focused on that dream.

What will go on your board? What is in your future that you need to visualize right now?

_____
_____
_____
_____
_____
_____
_____
_____
_____
_____
_____
_____
_____
_____
_____
_____

Displaying Your Vision – A Vision for Greater Influence through TV Appearances, Larger Venues

Debra in Texas shared a pretty radical approach for displaying her vision. I don't know that knocking out a wall is the right choice for everyone, but it is important to make sure you really commit to getting the vision and keeping it in front of you in whatever way is necessary to make sure you stay focused.

What radical steps do you need to take to make this vision a part of your daily life? Where do you need to put your vision board so it is sure to be a priority for you?

_____
_____
_____
_____
_____
_____
_____
_____
_____
_____
_____
_____
_____
_____
_____
_____

Once the Board Is Up – A Vision to See Greeting Cards in Gift Shops

Daria is a great example of how to go beyond creating a board and become proactive in visualizing goals. She understood that it takes more than putting pictures together and staring at them occasionally. She found ways to see herself accomplishing her dreams on a regular basis. And it worked!

In what ways can you see yourself accomplishing what is on your vision board?

The Law of Attraction at Work – A Vision for a Baby

Bethany in Virginia took a big risk when she began believing for her baby. She took steps that could have been heartbreaking for someone longing for a baby. Those around her might have asked, "What will you do with these things if the baby never comes?" or "Why would you open yourself up to potential pain?" But, she kept believing and kept speaking of this baby as if it were already here. She trusted that this was part of her future and the gift of her baby was even more blessed because she never gave up.

Are you exercising the Law of Attraction in how you speak about your dreams? What are you attracting into your life with your attitude and your faith?

Who Should See Your Dreams? – A Vision for a Husband, a House, and a Business

Diana S. shows us how surrounding yourself with people who support you in your dreams is essential to believing even in the face of discouragement and disappointment. She is a prime example of what happens when you are careful to share your dreams with those who will help you stay focused on your vision for your future.

Are you sharing your dreams with the right people? Have you had an experience where someone responded to your vision with negativity? How did you handle that situation?

What to Do While You're Waiting – A Vision for a Mission Trip and a Business

Tammy in Texas applied all of the principles for creating a vision, keeping it in front of you in the form of a vision board, and reviewing your goals regularly. She made a practice out of keeping her vision alive while she worked toward achieving her goals and trusting God's timing for them to come together.

What do you need to do while you are waiting? What can you do to be proactive and fulfill your part in bringing your dreams to fruition?

_____
_____
_____
_____
_____
_____
_____
_____
_____
_____
_____
_____
_____
_____
_____
_____
_____
_____

The Hidden Key – A Vision for a Significant Seed

Courtney of South Dakota has a remarkable story of sowing seeds for a specific goal. She took a brave step of faith and continued doing that even through great hardship. It paid off in miraculous ways and she has begun to see her vision come together.

What seeds are you sowing toward your dreams? Do you believe you can sow seeds that will benefit others and yourself?

_____
_____
_____
_____
_____
_____
_____
_____
_____
_____
_____
_____
_____
_____
_____
_____
_____
_____
_____
_____

APPENDIX
CELEBRATING THE VISION

Host a Vision Board Group or Party

Hosting a vision board small group or a one-night party can bring such fulfillment to your life. You, as the host, will be pivotal in helping others dismiss a life of stagnation and become energized to go after their dreams.

Begin by inviting some friends to embark on a life-changing journey of achieving their dreams. Depending on the duration of your vision board parties, whether it is a multiple-week small group gathering or a one-time party you plan to host, I have provided a format for both types of vision board gatherings to help you. Implement the format that works best for you and your desire for hosting these inspiring meetings.

Remember, vision boards are a starting point of dream achievement. They are not the end-all "magic" board that makes fairy-tale living possible. Vision board parties are useless and ineffective if they are simply turned into a "scrap-booking on a bulletin board" event. That's why I encourage follow-up gatherings more than just a one-time event, especially for people starting to learn about developing and pursuing their dreams and goals. The weekly group setting will allow you to encourage and influence each other to implement successful routines and behaviors that can bring about the desired results.

One of the greatest benefits of throwing a vision board party is the accountability it provides. Making a vision board sounds great and most people get inspired to locate their scissors and pick up a poster board; however, when it comes down to actually making the board, it can seem like a lot of work too. Getting together with others will crush procrastination and inspire you and your friends to take action.

Remember, a vision board is as unique as the individual designing it. It is simply a collection of pictures and words that describe each person's ideal future. Although I have expressed my personal style of listing my top ten goals for the year, as well as bigger aspirations that may occur over the next several years, there is not really a right or wrong way to design your board. Yours and your participant's boards might communicate their dreams for this year or for this decade. Choose what works best for each individual to keep them motivated on their fulfillment.

Just to reiterate why I choose to display my immediate annual goals is simply for the purpose of staying encouraged by their fulfillment as opposed to only displaying huge dreams that may require a ten-year span to acquire. It can be very demotivating to look at the same board for ten or twelve years and still see nothing achieved. I also like to have a personal vision board and a separate vision board for my ministry.

I've created a series of videos about the purpose of vision boards and how to use them effectively. Simply go to www.terri.com for access and to share them with your group to inspire them and start the countdown to your event.

Tips for Hosting Your Own Vision Board Small Group

Invite 6-12 people. Smaller groups like this help to create a comfortable environment for conversations, the ability to communicate dreams and goals, as well as give and receive encouragement.

Let them know about the vision board kits available from us at www.terri.com before you meet. This kit includes: *Dream It. Pin It. Live It.* book, *Dream It. Pin It. Live It.* workbook, one cork board, decorative push pins, some of my favorite motivational phrases, confessions, and Bible verses, all in a convenient carrying box. The book and workbook will serve as the learning map for your group.

Week 1: Welcome and discussion on chapters 1 and 2.
    Chapter 1: Give Yourself Permission to Dream
    Chapter 2: The Power of the Pen
        Assignment: Start the "101 Dreams" list. Encourage your group to write as many as they can without the pressure of finishing the list.

Week 2: Discuss writing "101 Dreams" assignment and chapters 3 and 4.
    Chapter 3: Your Top Ten Goals
    Chapter 4: Design Your Board
        Assignment: List your top ten goals for the next 12-18 months. Bring supplies for vision board party at the next gathering.

Week 3: Vision Board Party
        Have fun decorating and designing your boards together.

Week 4: Discuss chapters 5 and 6.
    Chapter 5: Display Your Destiny
    Chapter 6: Once the Board is Up

Week 5: Discuss chapters 7 and 8.
    Chapter 7: The Law of Attraction in Action
    Chapter 8: Don't Share Big Dreams with Small Minds

Week 6: Discuss chapters 9 and 10 and prayer
    Chapter 9: What to Do While You're Waiting
    Chapter 10: The Hidden Key to Living Your Dreams
        Pray over each person's dreams and goals.

Tips for Hosting a One-Night Vision Board Party

#1. Invite 6-12 people. Keep the guest list minimal in order to have room for guests to work on their vision boards. Larger groups can make it harder for those attending to share their dreams and goals. Encourage your guests to think about their dreams prior to the party.

#2. Let your group know about the vision board kits available from us at www.terri.com. If you are not planning to use our vision board kit, then encourage the participants to bring their own vision board to the party which could include a poster board, cork board or a magnetic board.

#3. Ask the participants to bring a collection of magazines, postcards, or brochures that they don't mind sharing and cutting into pieces. The more variety, the better.

#4. Personal photos. Using personal images on the board enables you to clearly see yourself living that dream. Ask guests to bring a variety of their own photographs to pin next to their goals.

#5. Additional items to request or provide: Glue, glitter, stickers, stamps, markers, motivational phrases, scrap-booking supplies (this can range from a broad variety of visuals such as "destination stickers" for those wanting to take a dream trip to miniature graduation caps symbolizing your dream of obtaining a college degree, etc).

#6. Every gathering is better with food! Whether you provide snacks, prepare a meal, or have everyone bring something to share, having something available to eat will help make your time together even better.

Have fun together. Inspire each other to travel to new places, explore new territories, learn a new language or skill, enroll in a class, and to dream big!

Encourage guests to not leave until at least three items are on their board. Many people will have great intentions and truly want to finish their board once they get home, but the reality is, months will pass by with the board unfinished and dreams still unrealized. They can always add to it, but having at least three top goals to pursue is a great place to start.

Remind your participants that their vision board is a visual reminder of where they intend to be. This activity is for the purpose of identifying their true dreams and clarifying their immediate goals. This is a powerful tool to help your goals become more tangible and focused. This visual imagery enables you to see yourself living the dreams, plans, and purposes God's given you.

VISION BOARD SAMPLES
A Variety of Dreams Displayed

1ST CAR
SPEED LIMIT 50
I ♥ NY
learn the guitar
BUY A HORSE!
CONCERT TICKETS
SALE
JOY
ride

Santorini Greece
SABA
2015 FIAT 500
Je suis une femme complète, accomplie,
et épanouie!
Je suis une femme bénie!
GOLD WINNER
Twin Boy & Girl
award-winning Children's book author
book launch
EBONY TALK RADIO
WOMEN OF INFLUENCE
CAMP

A YEAR FROM NOW YOU WILL WISH YOU HAD STARTED TODAY
Karen Lamb
The NEW me
135 134 133 132
131 130 129 128
127 126 125 124
123 122 121 120
119 118 117 116
115 114 113 112
111 I DID it!! 110
FAST FOOD
"UNLESS YOU PUKE, FAINT, OR DIE, KEEP GOING"
NOTHING TASTES AS GOOD AS SKINNY FEELS
YOU CAN'T EXPECT TO LOOK LIKE A MILLION BUCKS IF YOU EAT FROM THE DOLLAR MENU
"THE FAT YOU EAT IS THE FAT YOU WEAR"

VISION
PASSPORT
USA
mission trip
NEW!
New Car
Vacation

GRATITUDE JOURNAL